Laurence Hutton

Literary Landmarks of Rome

Laurence Hutton

Literary Landmarks of Rome

ISBN/EAN: 9783744777889

Printed in Europe, USA, Canada, Australia, Japan

Cover: Foto ©Thomas Meinert / pixelio.de

More available books at **www.hansebooks.com**

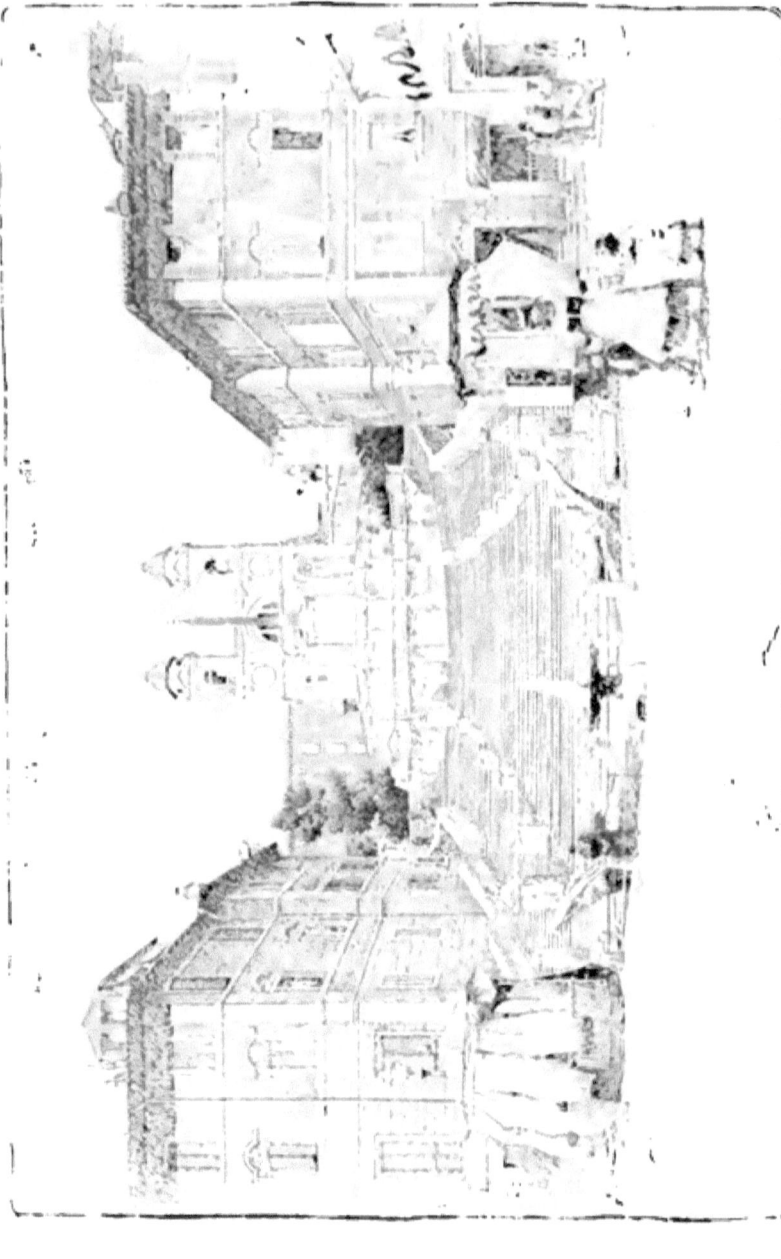

HOUSE IN WHICH KEATS DIED

THE SPANISH STEPS

HOUSE IN WHICH SHELLEY LIVED

LITERARY LANDMARKS

OF

ROME

BY

LAURENCE HUTTON

AUTHOR OF "LITERARY LANDMARKS OF FLORENCE"
"LITERARY LANDMARKS OF VENICE"
ETC., ETC.

ILLUSTRATED

NEW YORK
HARPER & BROTHERS PUBLISHERS

TO
EDMUND CLARENCE STEDMAN
THE EARLIEST PERSONAL LANDMARK
IN
MY LITERARY LIFE

ILLUSTRATIONS

THE SPANISH STEPS	*Frontispiece*	
POMPEY'S STATUE	*Facing p.*	8
THE FORUM	"	12
ALBERGO DELL' ORSO	"	18
TASSO'S GARDEN	"	20
SANTA MARIA SOPRA MINERVA	"	22
KEATS'S GRAVE	"	34
SHELLEY'S GRAVE	"	40
CONSTANCE FENIMORE WOOLSON'S GRAVE	"	42
THE HOUSE OF ANDERSEN, PIAZZA BARBERINI	"	46
HILDA'S TOWER	"	64

LITERARY LANDMARKS OF ROME

LITERARY LANDMARKS OF ROME

ROME, like Venice, is merely the stopping-place of the modern Man of Letters. Florence is his home. He lives in Florence; he lodges here. In Florence he buys a villa, or he takes a long lease of a house; and sometimes he engages a plot in the Protestant Cemetery; in Rome he usually stays at a hotel, or he makes *pension* arrangements for a limited period. If he dies in Rome he sometimes leaves here only a portion of his anatomy, and he sends his heart, or his ashes, to be buried somewhere else.

There are two distinct classes of English-speaking visitors to Rome, each of whom, no doubt, are willing to learn something, and to see something, of its Literary Landmarks.

The first of these have read Ruskin and Mrs. Jameson. They think they know all about art; while, unlike Mr. Vedder's beasts of the fields, in too many instances, they do not even know what they like. They sit for hours in rapt enthusiasm before "The Last Judgment" or before the "Apollo Belvedere," looking at those masterpieces through little, temporary opera-glasses made of their own fingers, or holding up their right hands and wagging their right thumbs, in that peculiar manner which is supposed to denote high-art appreciation, and which must be familiar to all students of the students of art. They gather a great deal of satisfaction out of Rome, and they go away from it perfectly content with their own familiarity with all its rich artistic treasures. The second class of visitors skim through the galleries and the churches of Rome as if on parlor-skates, and in a bored-to-death-sick-and-tired-of-the-Old-Masters sort of way, which is as sincere as it is self-evident and is ingenuously expressed. They are always heartily thankful when it is all over, and they utter a sigh of absolute relief when they learn that they have gone somewhere on the wrong day, and have absolutely no other day on which to go. For both these classes — traditional sight-seers both, and both of them worthy of all respect — is here given some idea of what the men who made Rome did in Rome, and of how and where they did it, from Cicero and Cæsar to Shelley and Keats, in the hope and belief that the tourist will get as much out of Horace and Hawthorne in Rome as out of Raphael and Salvator Rosa, or out of Donatello and Carlo Dolci.

It is, of course, no longer possible to point out the exact Landmarks of the Literary Romans of twenty centuries ago, when Balbus and his mysterious contemporary — a gentleman always addressed as "Thou" — were accustomed to lift up their hands, for some unknown and seemingly utterly useless reason, and to the great confusion of our tenses, persons, and numbers in our Latin Prose Compositions. Cicero and Tacitus, and Cato and Sallust, and even Julius Cæsar, have left but few footprints on the sands of Rome; and these Darwin's obliterating earth-worm and the ravages of Time have wiped out almost entirely.

Not pretending to any knowledge of antiquarian lore, the present literary pilgrim, in this portion of his narrative, must depend upon the antiquarian knowledge of Mr. Augustus J. C. Hare, of Dr. S. Russell Forbes, of the late Professor J. Henry Middleton, and of Signor Rodolfo Lanciani; only adding that he himself has seen, or has tried to see, everything which they point out, and that he sees, and has attempted to see, no reason to doubt the truth of their researches. Without their aid he would have been lost in ancient Rome; and to them he begs to extend here his most sincere thanks.

Dr. Forbes believes that Cicero's house, under the Palatine, was above that of Cæsar; that Cicero made his first oration against Catiline in the Temple of Jupiter Stator, at the foot of the Palatine Hill, and he places Cicero's Tusculan Villa on the site of what is now a Greek monastery, the Grotta Ferrata. He adds that Cicero mentions statues of the Muses which stood in his library, and that these statues were actually found there many centuries later. It was here that Cicero laid the scenes of his *De Divinatione* and *Tusculanæ Disputationes;* and here he received the news of his proscription.

It is also recorded that Cicero was more than once entertained by Lucullus in that famous villa which stood on the southwestern side of the Pincian Hill; and that upon his return from banishment, fifty-seven years before the beginning of the Christian Era, he was received in triumph by the Senate and the People of Rome (S. P. Q. R.) at the Porta Capena, on the Appian Way.

After his assassination the head and the hands of Cicero were placed upon the Rostra, a temporary structure which stood in the Forum in front of the Curia, where it is recorded that Fulvia, the widow of Clodius, spat in his dead face, and added injury to insult, in a truly unfeminine way, but with a truly feminine weapon, by sticking her hairpin through his speechless tongue.

All students will remember that Julius

Cæsar announced that all Gaul was divided into three parts, each of which, with all the gall in his possession, he attached to himself. This celebrated Man of Letters, against the advice of his wife, Calpurnia, went out to meet his fate on a famous March morning, from the Regia, close to the Temple of Vesta in the Forum; and here his widow received his body, brought back with all its gaping wounds by a few of his faithful slaves. Alas! it was too late for her to tell him that she had told him so; but no doubt, in all her great grief, she thought it.

Mr. Forbes says that Cæsar lived in the first house in the Via Sacra. He describes it as fronting towards the Temple of Vesta; while the portico and shops, built at a later period over its ruins, ran parallel with the Sacred Way. The house-side of the atrium, he continues, is plainly marked by the fragments of columns, composed of travertine coated with stucco and frescoed; and amidst the shops are remains of a beautiful black and white mosaic pavement, the fragments of the borders showing that they once belonged to the older edifice. The mansion had two entrances into the Via Sacra, one nearly touching its northeastern corner.

Cæsar was not killed in the Capitol, as Shakspere said. What Hamlet called that Brute part was played in Pompey's Senate House, or the Theatre of Pompey — the church of S. Andrea della Valle, on the new thoroughfare called Corso Vittorio Emanuele, now standing upon its site. Mr. Forbes explains that the great star beneath the cupola marks, as nearly as possible, the spot upon which the autocrat fell. As the deposed Bonaparte lies under the dome of the Invalides, in Paris, so rises, in Rome, a dome over the place where another, if not a greater, conqueror was extinguished.

Pompey's Statue, a colossal, not ungainly figure of a man, at the feet of which great Cæsar fell, is believed generally to be now standing in the Palazzo Spada alla Regola, in the Piazza Capo di Ferro. It is placed in what is called the council-chamber of the palace; and what are said to be the stains of great Cæsar's blood are still visible upon the calf of Pompey's left leg. Mr. Hare quotes Suetonius as narrating that the statue "was removed from the Curia by Augustus, and placed upon a marble Janus in front of the basilica"; and the same authority—Mr. Hare—adds that "it was found upon that exact spot during the pontificate of Julius III." [1550-55]. Whether this be the original figure of Pompey or not, it has been addressed by Byron as "Thou dread statue! yet existent in the austerest form of naked mystery"; and it has been accepted and apostrophized by many other well-known writers of prose and of verse as being authentic. And while I am willing to accept it myself, I must put myself on record as doubting somewhat the stains of Cæsar's blood.

Although the art treasures of the Spada Palace are not visible to-day, except by special permission of the existing head of the Spada family, the porter at the gate will, for a small gratuity, admit the stranger to the hall upon the second floor where the dread statue stands. And it is worth re-

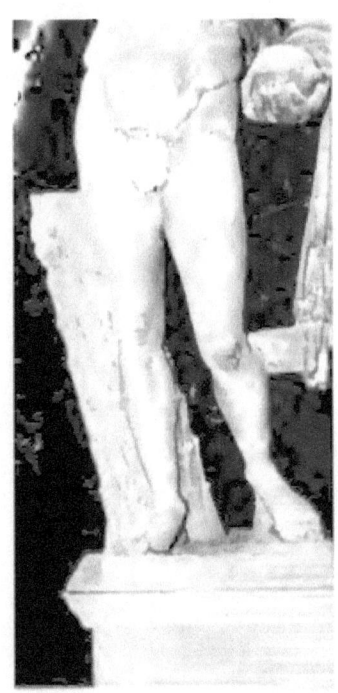

POMPEY'S STATUE

cording, as an interesting and characteristic fact, that the French in the winter of 1788–89 carried this figure to the Colosseum, where they enacted Voltaire's tragedy of *Brutus*, in accents unborn in Brutus's time, and where they murdered Cæsar once more at its base. This was a performance which could only have been equalled by the entertainment which Colonel William F. Cody, with his Wild West Show, wished to give, a century later, on the same spot.

"The statue is entirely nude," said Hawthorne, "except for a cloak that hangs down from the left shoulder; in the left hand is held a globe; the right arm is extended. The whole expression is such as the statue might have assumed, if, during the tumult of Cæsar's murder, it had stretched forth its marble hand and motioned the conspirators to give over the attack, or to be quiet, now that their victim had fallen at its feet. On the left leg, about midway above the ankle, there is a dull red stain, said to be Cæsar's blood; but, of course, it is just such a red stain in the marble as may be seen on the statue of Antinous at the Capitol. . . . I am glad to have seen this statue, and glad to remember it in that gray, dim, lofty hall; glad that there were no bright frescos on the walls, and that the ceiling was wrought with massive beams and the floor paved with ancient brick."

Mark Antony delivered his famous funeral oration on the Rostra Julia, on the eastern side of the Forum. The ancient writers tell us how greatly it moved the people, who immediately burned the body in that very place, and afterwards interred the ashes there; but they do not report Antony's words. That they could hardly be more moving than were the words put into Antony's mouth by Shakspere all reporters of great speeches, in the present day, must assuredly admit. The Temple of Cæsar, which was erected on his funeral pile, Signor Lanciani says, was destroyed in 1546. It is now an unmarked mass of rough and broken stones.

The Temple of Cæsar and Cæsar's house, and the other intensely interesting features of the Forum, are not easily distinguished by the present pilgrim, even with the aid of the clearest of plans. Small tablets stating "Here Cæsar Lived" or "Here Cæsar Died," or here happened this, or here happened that, historical event, would be of great help to the inquiring tourist of to-day. If Keats and Scott and Goethe are so honored by the municipality of Rome, why should not the homes of the men of earlier times have some mark to distinguish their occupancy?

Very few spots in the world are more impressive than is this same Roman Forum. Here one walks, by means of a few modern wooden steps, out of the End of the Nineteenth Century into a space dating back to a period when there were no centuries at all, as we count them; to a period which was old before the Middle Ages were born. And in the Forum, even more strongly than at the Pyramids themselves, is one forced to acknowledge that art is short, and that time is fleeting.

The villa and the gardens of Sallust, a

literary gentleman not unknown to the students of the dead languages in the high-schools of most living countries, Professor Middleton placed in the Barberini Villa gardens, in the valley between the Quirinal and the Pincian Hills. It was probably destroyed, he said, in the fire of 410, but he traced certain portions of it which are still remaining; and he described a nobly designed hall once lined with rich marble, and decorated with statues, handsome staircases, and the like. Its site is gradually being covered with the brand-new buildings which are fast making this part of Rome as modern as is modern New York or modern Paris. It is approached by horse-cars, it is lighted by electricity, and it is surrounded by hotels, which look like the Fifth Avenue and the Continental, and are quite as comfortable and quite as expensive as are these familiar hostelries of modern times.

Virgil is said to have lived on the Esquiline Hill, near the gardens of Mæcenas; and Horace is known to have been a constant guest in the villa of Mæcenas, which he

THE FORUM

has frequently described. Signor Lanciani points out the very interesting fact that Horace bought his books of the dealers in ancient and modern literature who did business in the Argiletum, a quarter situated between the Roman Forum and the Suburra, and corresponding to the Paternoster Row or the Nassau Street of modern literary towns.

The authorities agree that Mæcenas, whose hospitality has become proverbial, entertained the poets of the Augustan Age in a house which stood upon the Esquiline Hill, where the Baths of Titus were afterwards placed; Mr. Forbes adding the interesting fact that the amiable and harmonic Nero saw the burning of Rome, to the slow music of his own violin, from a tower of this villa.

Pliny is supposed to have lived on the summit of the Vicus Cyprius, probably on the Via S. Maria Maggiore, in a little house previously occupied by another poet, one Pedo Albinovanus. The exact site of this house is not known now, and the majority of the authorities do not mention it at all.

Petrarch is said to have been a guest of

the head of the Colonna family during at least one of his visits to Rome; but as the present palace bearing the Colonna name is a century later than the time of Petrarch, the poet naturally could not have known it. It stands not far from the site of the ancient fortress which the earlier Colonnas occupied, and perhaps Petrarch went from this fortress, in 1341, to receive the laurel crown in the great Senate Hall on the Capitol Hill. He had much to say about Rome and about what seemed to him its decadence. He found here neither repose nor content; civil and foreign wars were desolating the land; houses were sinking; walls were falling to the ground; temples and shrines were yielding to decay; laws were trampled under foot; justice was a prey to violence; and the unhappy people sighed and groaned; all because Pope Urban V. was at Avignon, and there were no good Humbert and charming Margaret, with their strong common-sense and their kindliness of heart, to make Rome what it is to-day, a city of peace and of outward prosperity, wisely and justly governed, and occupied by a people happy and well pleased with themselves and with their rulers.

Luther came to Rome when he was twenty-seven or twenty-eight years of age, and he remained here but two short weeks. No man ever hated Rome as Luther hated it, not for itself, but for its influences; and during the rest of his life he wrote and spoke of Rome in the strongest terms of disgust and condemnation. Rome thoroughly weaned him from Rome, and made him the Pope of the Heretics of his time. And out of Rome he carried nothing that was comforting, except the feeling that if he had not had his fortnight in Rome he never would have believed that Rome and the Romans could be half so bad as he was now convinced they were. His thoughts and reflections upon the Eternal City, therefore, can hardly be recommended as sympathetic reading-matter to the enthusiastic pilgrims of the present time.

Luther while here was an inhabitant of the Augustine Convent, adjoining the church of S. Maria del Popolo; and he is said to have occupied the rooms which are now the offices of the Director of the Parks and Gardens of Rome. They are, of course, entirely changed, in furniture and in appearance, since Luther's day.

Mr. Hare, who quotes so happily always, quotes the author of *The Schönberg-Cotta Chronicles* as describing how Luther, on his knees, as is the invariable rule, climbed, painfully, up the Holy Staircase, or the "Scala Santa"; "when he suddenly stood erect, lifted his face heavenward, and in another instant turned and walked slowly and deliberately down again." This was a way of Luther's throughout life; and if the story be true—it seems to be founded on fact—Luther's are the only feet which have touched those holy steps since the days of Pontius Pilate; when, says tradition, they were trod—in Pilate's house at Jerusalem—by the sacred feet of the Messiah Himself. They are now covered with boards, beneath which, however, the original marble—said to be Italian marble—is still visible; and at all hours of the day, and on every day of the week, pilgrims of all ages, of both sexes, and of every condition of life, babies and agèd persons, beggars and princes, side by side, may be seen toiling painfully on their knees from the bottom to the top, saying a prayer on every one of the twenty-eight steps. Concerning the divine association of these steps tradition only can be relied upon, but millions of earnest Christians, Luther among them, have made their ascent during the hundreds of years in which they have been where they are; and they are of great interest now, for Luther's sake, if for no other.

The register of the Albergo dell' Orso, if that once famous Bear Hotel ever had a register, would be not only of enormous value, as a collection of autographs, but of great help to the literary pilgrim in Rome to-day. The inn stood for centuries on the same spot, in the Via dell' Orso; it was always in the hotel business, central, commanding, fashionable, and comfortable, as the advertisements would say; and, in the height of its glory and prosperity, it entertained guests of the greatest distinction in all walks of life, and from all parts of the globe. Montaigne slept under its roof, and it is even claimed for it that Dante made it his home when he came—if he ever did come—as the Ambassador of Florence to the Pope of Rome, at the beginning of the Fourteenth Century; although this is mere conjecture. The building condemned to demolition still stood, in its shabby old age, frequented by peasants, when I last saw it; but it was entirely unnoticed by the hundreds of thousands of tourists who passed it on their way to and from St. Peter's. Its massive vaults and fine old columns were once the delight of the artists. And Lord Herbert of Cherbury mentioned it, fondly, in more than one of his letters.

Montaigne kept a journal of his adventures in, and his impressions of, Rome during his stay here in the winter of 1580–81. He regretted that nothing was left of ancient Rome but the sky above it and the outline of its form; but he was delighted with its climate and its society; and he confessed

ALBERGO DELL' ORSO

that he had never breathed air more temperate or better suited to his constitution. This latter, it may be remarked, could not have been written truthfully during many of the winter months of the last few years.

Montaigne arrived in Rome on the 30th November, 1580, and went to the Bear, where he stayed that day and the next, but on the 2d December he hired apartments at the house of a Spaniard opposite the church of S. Lucia della Tinta, where he was provided with three handsome bedrooms, a dining-room, a closet, stable, and kitchen, for twenty crowns a month, the landlord including in that sum a cook and fire for the kitchen. He had an audience with the Pope, witnessed the execution of Catena, a famous robber and captain of banditti, which he called "a spectacle," and he found the winter nearly as cold as that of Gascony. His account of one of the many sights he saw is worth quoting in full. "On Easter Eve," he said, "I went to see, at S. John Lateran, the heads of S. Paul and S. Peter, which are exhibited there on that day. The heads are entire, with the hair, flesh, color, and beard as if they still lived. S. Peter has a long face, with a brilliant complexion approaching the sanguine, with a gray picked beard, and a papal mitre on his head. S. Paul is of a dark complexion, with a broader and fuller face, a large head, and a thick gray beard."

Tasso died, and was buried, in 1595, in the monastery of S. Onofrio, on the side of the Janiculum, a hill rising above the right bank of the Tiber, where he sought refuge and rest and the laurel crown. Refuge and rest he found; but the crown was not placed upon his brow until his life had ebbed away. His room, containing his relics, and a mask, in wax, of his dead face, suffered so much from the great powder explosion which shook all Rome a few years ago that it has been closed by order of the government, has been sealed with the seals of the city, and is no longer shown to the public. Tasso was originally buried on the left side of the convent church, under an altar-tomb containing his painted portrait and a Latin inscription, which still remain. But, in 1857, his bones

TASSO'S GARDEN

were removed to an adjoining chapel, where, under a more magnificent tomb, ornamented by a marble statue, they now lie.

In the convent garden still stands a son of "Tasso's Oak," the tree which the poet himself planted there having ended its long life in a disastrous gale some half-century ago. In this beautiful garden Tasso was fond of sitting, when the weather and his feeble health permitted, with a beautiful vista of old Rome at his feet, and with the Alban and the Sabine hills beyond. The monks are still very proud of their association with the great Italian; and the barefooted, bareheaded brother who took us through the church one bright December day suggested so strongly, in personal appearance and in voice, Mr. Francis Wilson, the comedian, that we felt as if we were assisting at the representation of a new drama, in which the well-known actor was, for the first time, playing a serious part, and playing it with rare skill and tender, tragic feeling.

Galileo was tried in the Convent of S. Maria sopra Minerva here, in the Piazza della Minerva, a Christian church erected in the Thirteenth Century upon the ruins of a temple to the heathen goddess whose name, in part, it bears. He was conveyed to Rome from Florence in the depths of a heavy winter—and winter between Florence and Rome can be heavy enough, when it is so determined—and he was, probably, tortured for persisting in the statement that the world goes round. That it has gone round far enough to realize that Galileo was right is now universally acknowledged.

Milton, after leaving Galileo in Florence, spent some time in Rome in the autumn of 1638, " detained here by the antiquity and ancient renown of the city." Unfortunately he left no record of his impressions here, or of what he did or saw. He is perhaps the only Man of Letters who ever visited the Eternal City without telling, in prose, to the world what he thought about it; and his pictures of Rome written in *Paradise Regained* might have been the work of a man who had never seen Rome at all. George S. Hillard said

SANTA MARIA SOPRA MINERVA

that Milton "was received by Cardinal Barberini in an unpretending house with many green blinds, in the Via Quattro Fontane, at the corner made by the street which leads from the Quirinal Palace to the Porta Pia," and that there he saw and heard Leonora Baroni, who was the Patti of her day, and who pleased him so greatly by her vocal and personal charms that he indited to her eyebrows no less than three Latin epigrams.

"I must not forget," wrote Hawthorne, in 1858, "that on our way from the Barberini Palace we stopped an instant to look at the house at the corner of the Street of the Four Fountains where Milton was a guest while in Rome. He seems quite a man of our own day, seen so nearly at the hither extremity of the vista through which we look back. The house (it was then occupied by the Cardinal Barberini) looks as if it might have been built in the present century."

There is a tradition that Milton, despite his advanced Puritanism, was entertained sumptuously by the monks in the English

College at Rome on the 31st October, 1638.

John Evelyn wrote in his *Diary:* "I came to Rome on the 4th November, 1644, about five at night; and being perplexed for a convenient lodging, wandered up and down on horseback, till at last one conducted us to Monsieur Petit's, a Frenchman, near the Piazza Spagnola [*sic*]. Here I alighted, and having bargained with my host for twenty crowns a month, I caused a good fire to be made in my chamber, and went to bed being so very wet. The next morning (for I was determined to spend no time idly here) I got acquainted with several persons who have long lived in Rome. . . . In the first place, our sights-man (for so they name certain persons here who get their living by leading strangers about to see the city) went to the Palace Farnese," etc., etc. And so saw Evelyn all the sights in the true tourist's way, his sights-man carrying him to look at everything which we who have come after him, for two centuries and a half, have conscientiously " done."

He left Rome for a tour through the neighboring country, and returned on the 13th February, 1645. On the 18th May he wrote, " Having taken leave of our friends at Rome, where I had sojourned now about seven months, autumn, winter, and spring, I took coach with two courteous Italian gentlemen." There is no room to record here his feelings or impressions. But to Evelyn, as to all the rest of us, since Rome was, Rome was—Rome!

Gray, who was in Rome in 1739–40, confessed that the magnificence of the city far exceeded his expectation of it. He entered by the gate of the Piazza del Popolo, and spoke with enthusiasm of the views in every street or square, which he declared the most picturesque and noble ever imagined. He was the companion of Horace Walpole, but neither of them gave any of the particulars of his visit, except that Walpole wrote: " How I like the inanimate part of Rome you will soon perceive at my arrival in England. I am far gone in medals, lamps, idols, prints, and all the small commodities to the purchase of which I can attain. I would buy the Colosseum if I could."

Smollett lived in the Piazza di Spagna in 1765, where for a decent first floor, and for two bedrooms on the second floor, he paid no more than one scudo *per diem*.

During Goethe's visit to Rome in 1786 he lived in an apartment in the long house numbered 15 to 20 Via del Corso, a few doors from the Piazza del Popolo end of that thoroughfare, and on the western side of the way. The entrance is at No. 18 Via del Corso, and the tablet commemorating Goethe's occupancy is under the second-story window of No. 20. Of his experiences here he wrote that he was at last living in serenity and in peace; his acquired habit of seeing and interpreting all things as they are, his fidelity in keeping the eye light, his complete renunciation of all pretension standing him in good stead, according to his own statement, and making him tranquilly and deeply happy. He certainly saw all things that Rome had to show him, in the way of palaces and ruins, gardens and wastes, triumphal arches, columns, and cathedrals, and he interpreted them all in his own way. No doubt he kept his eye light, and he unquestionably renounced all pretension, by what he called "an odd and perhaps whimsical half-incognito," which seems to have deceived nobody but himself, and to have had no effect whatever upon anybody. His self-imposed title was "The-man-who-lives-across-the-way-from-the-Rondinini-Palace"; and as such he fancied that he had managed to escape the endless inconvenience of being obliged to give an account of himself and of his wonderful performances. What the Romans thought of him then—he was only thirty-seven years of age—and of his *Sorrows of Young Werther*, his complete renunciation of all pretension, alas! will never permit us to know.

Hillard said, and very prettily, that "Goethe painted Rome while Châteaubriand set it to music"; and he translated Châteaubriand's "sonata" on "Rome by Moonlight," which is well worth quoting here: "Rome is asleep in the midst of her ruins. This star of the night, this orb which is supposed to be extinguished and unpeopled, moves through her pale solitudes, above the solitude of Rome. She shines upon the streets without inhabitants, upon enclosed spaces, open squares, and gardens in which no one walks, upon monasteries where the voices of monks are no longer heard, upon cloisters which are as deserted as the arches of the Colosseum." Read this by the light of the moon in Rome, and it will soothe one's breast, no matter how savage it may be against the beggary and wretchedness and extortions of some of the persons who dwell in Rome to-night.

Bonaparte sent Châteaubriand to Rome as Secretary of Legation in 1803, and he lived, no doubt, in the Palace of Cardinal Fesch, the French Ambassador.

Those of us who have wept over the woes of Virginius as Sheridan Knowles put them into blank verse, and as Forrest and McCullough made them seem so real to us on the mimic stage, will feel a certain sensation of interest in standing opposite the shrine of Venus, at the corner of the Vicus Tuscus and the Via Sacra, where stood the butcher's stall from which came the knife that took Virginia's life and saved her honor. Dr. Forbes says that "facing up the Vicus Tuscus is some brickwork—remains of a line of shops that faced towards the Temple of Cæsar." The end shop alone was saved when the excavations were recently made, and on its site the butcher sold his meat and kept his cleavers.

Tradition says, by-the-way, but only tradition and no one else, that Virginia was buried on Mons Sacer, a couple of miles beyond the Porta Pia; and there still exists there a tomb which is said to be hers. Macaulay, in verse, has told the story of her funeral, and Dionysius gave a long account of its magnificence and pomp, and of the crowds of citizens who attended it; but it is not positively known now where—

"They brought a bier, and hung it with many a cypress crown;
And gently they uplifted her, and gently laid her down."

Speaking of Macaulay, it may not be amiss

to say that the Bridge which Horatius kept so well in the brave days of old was the Sublician Bridge, a little below the spot where the Ponte Rotto now spans the Tiber. It is no longer standing, although certain of its wooden piers can be distinguished when the tide of the Tiber is unusually low.

"I then went down the river," wrote Macaulay himself, in his *Journal*, 16th November, 1838, "to the spot where the old Pons Sublicius stood, and looked about to see how my 'Horatius' agreed with the topography. Pretty well: but his house must be on Mount Palatine, for he would never see Mount Cœlius from the spot where he fought." Macaulay does not say where was his own house while he stayed in Rome.

Corinne was, unquestionably, the result of Madame de Staël's visit to Italy in 1804, and the chapters of it which are descriptive of Rome, as she saw it, should not be overlooked by those who want to see Rome through all sorts and conditions of eyes.

Rogers wrote, in 1814: "We dwell among the clouds and look down on the Seven Hills of Rome. We are in the Rondinini Palace, distinguished for the possession of the celebrated mask of the Medusa, and from its windows we command a little world." The Rondinini Palace is now numbered 518 Via del Corso, and is nearly opposite the one-time lodging-place of Goethe; but the "Rondinini Medusa" has been removed to Munich.

Rogers records some of his social experiences during his first visit here; he attended concerts at Lucian Bonaparte's palace, dined at Lord Holland's, visited Canova and Thorwaldsen, and had an audience with the Pope. He lived for a time in the Via Vittoria, close to the Via S. Maria de' Fiori; but in the later years of his life he occupied while in Rome a house in the Via Magenta, near the Piazza dell' Indipendenza.

Byron seems to have spent but little more than a fortnight in Rome, in May, 1817. "Of Rome," he wrote to Moore, "I say nothing. It is quite indescribable. . . . I have been on horseback most of the day all days since my arrival. . . . I have seen the

Pope alive, and a cardinal dead — both of whom looked very well indeed." And that is all. He was too eager to return to the Venice of his affections and evil doings to remain longer here. Byron lodged in the three-story double house, now numbered 84 and 85 Piazza di Spagna, on the corner of the Via Carrozza. His rooms were on an upper floor, and his windows looked out upon the Piazza towards the houses of Keats and Shelley, almost directly opposite. His last night in Rome was spent, it is said, in the Villa Mills, on the Palatine, now a convent of French nuns.

It is almost as difficult to-day, even at this comparatively short period of intervening time, to discover the Roman habitations of the Literary Men and Women of the present century as it is to identify the homes and the haunts of the men of the past. The memorial tablets, compared with those of Florence, are very few; and in biographies and autobiographies, in published *Letters* and *Journals*, very rarely are definite addresses given. Even the older residents of

Rome who remember Rogers and Hawthorne, Longfellow and Thackeray, here, do not remember where they lived. Miss Harriet Hosmer, most cheerful and entertaining of companions, most faithful of friends, forgets nothing, however; and to her kindly interest in my work, and to her affectionate regard for many of the men to whom it relates, I owe much of the valuable information I am able to present.

At No. 26 Piazza di Spagna, on the southern side of the famous steps leading up to the terrace of the Church of S. Trinità de' Monti, stands one of the most familiar of the Literary Landmarks of Rome. Immediately over the steps is a tablet stating, in Italian and in English, that in this house, on the 24th February, 1821, and at the age of twenty-six, died the young British poet John Keats. His rooms were directly below the tablet, and the modest building is situated in the very centre of what is called " The Strangers' Quarter " of Rome. The famous Piazza is near all the banks and the circulating libraries, it contains many of the popular hotels, and it is a scene of unending life, bustle, and activity. The army of Italy, blowing its own trumpet, passes and repasses almost every hour of the day; and at one end of the square rises the tall column erected in honor of the Establishment of the Immaculate Conception of the Virgin, with its colossal statue of the Holy Mother looking benignly down upon it all. Here one sees, among the people, a very curious commingling of past and of present, of the wildly picturesque and of the ugly commonplace; venders of brilliant flowers; priests and beggars; tweed-suited tourists; sheepskin-coated peasants; professional models, waiting to be hired, and arrayed in those fantastic colors which the painters of Rome represent so often; and professional cab-drivers and map-sellers dressed in garments which no artist would ever care to paint. Everything is delightfully strange and curiously familiar; and one instinctively feels, as Dickens felt, when he first arrived in Rome, that the models are all personal acquaintances whom he has met scores of times before, until he realizes that he has

KEATS'S GRAVE

seen their lineaments and their habiliments in every picture of Rome that was ever publicly exhibited in England or America. The models are as much a part of Rome as is St. Peter's or the Colosseum, and they are precisely what one expects them to be. The Pope's Guards, on the other side of the river, are, however, a bitter disappointment when seen in the winter months. The Papal authorities have covered the Fifteenth-Century Michael-Angelesque, red-and-yellow legs of their uniformed defenders with long, blue, modern American army sack-overcoats; and they appear now, to the untrained eye, as absurd as would seem the Jack of Clubs in an ulster!

The sad and harrowing story of Keats's last hours in Rome need not be repeated here. His friend Joseph Severn has told it all. Early in the month of October, 1820, Severn and Keats arrived together in Rome. Dr. Clark, afterwards Sir James Clark, found apartments for them in the building described above. "This," wrote Severn, " had the great advantage not only of good situation, but of being opposite to the physician's own house, which, indeed, was a prearrangement, so that Dr. Clark might have his patient near at all hours. We both found accommodations in the same house, and Keats's bedroom was the one which looked over the steps on the side of the house." On the 14th February, 1821, Severn wrote to Mrs. Brawne: "Little or no change has taken place in Keats since the commencement of this, except this beautiful one that his mind is growing to great quietness and peace;—I find this change has its rise from the increasing weakness of his body, but it seems like a delightful sleep to me. . . . Among the many things that he has requested of me to-night, this is the principal, that on his grave shall be this:

'Here lies one whose name was writ in water.'"

"At times during his last days," said Severn elsewhere, "he made me go to see the place where he was to be buried, and he expressed pleasure at my description of the locality of the Pyramid of Caius Cestius, about the grass and the many flowers, particularly the innumerable violets; also about the flock of goats and sheep and a young shepherd—all these intensely interested him. Violets were his favorite flowers, and he joyed to hear how they overspread the graves. He assured me that 'he had already seemed to feel the flowers growing over him.'" "And there they do grow," added Lord Houghton many months afterwards, "even all the winter long—violets and daisies mingling with the fresh herbage, and, in the words of Shelley, 'making one in love with death to think that one should be buried in so sweet a place.'"

Sixty-one years after the death of Keats, Severn himself was laid to rest by the side of the friend he had loved so well and had never forgotten.

Keats lies in the old portion of the Protestant Cemetery, very near the entrance. The monument, bearing a medallion portrait of him, has this inscription: "This grave contains all that was mortal of a young English poet who, on his death-bed, in the bitterness of his heart at the malicious power of his enemies, desired these words to be engraved upon his tombstone:

'Here lies one whose name was writ in water.'"

There are more numbers than there are houses in Rome, and almost as many tablets. Many houses have two numbers, some houses have three, and one particular house in the Via del Tritone is distinguished by no less than six; tablets being set up in some instances to mark ownership of the property, fire-insurance, business connections, divine interposition, and heroic occupancy, all over the same front door. This, naturally, is confusing. Shelley's house in the Piazza di Spagna has two numbers—25, which shows that it is next door to 24, and 366 in small blue figures; the reason for, or the meaning of, the latter being unknown to any person in the neighborhood, although they are generally supposed to have something to do with the gas or the water. The building has three tablets showing that fire policies are placed upon it in as many companies, and innumerable commercial signs; but there is nothing to explain that it was once the house of Shelley, as Mr. Forbes declares it to have been. It stands north of the house of Keats, with which it is almost identical in architecture, and on the other side of the famous steps.

Shelley wrote portions of *The Cenci* and of *Prometheus Unbound* in the Palazzo Verospi, Nos. 373, 374 Via del Corso. It is a great building in the busiest part of that thoroughfare — one of the Great Streets of the World — and a tablet recording Shelley's association with it was placed upon its front in the summer of 1893.

Shelley obtained these lodgings in the Palazzo Verospi in February, 1819, and there, in June, William Shelley, his son, died. The child was laid in the Protestant Cemetery, but exactly where is unknown. The tombstone erected to his memory was placed, in the absence of his parents, over the wrong grave.

Shelley's body was burned where it was found. His ashes were brought to Rome, but his heart, which the fire did not consume, given by Edward John Trelawney to Leigh Hunt, and by him surrendered to Mrs. Shelley, was carried with her to England, and is said to be still preserved, with other sacred relics of the poet and his wife, in Boscombe Manor, Bournemouth.

The tomb of Shelley is in the Protestant Cemetery, in the upper or eastern part of the new ground. It bears the name, the date of his birth and death, and the inscription "*Cor Cordium*," with the lines from *The Tempest*:

> "Nothing of him that doth fade,
> But doth suffer a sea change
> Into something rich and strange."

"A spot that touched me deeply," wrote George Eliot, in 1860, "was Shelley's grave. The English Cemetery in which he lies is the most attractive burial-place I have ever seen. It lies against the Old City walls close to the Porta S. Paolo, and is one of the quietest spots of Old Rome. And there, under the shadow of the old walls on one side and

SHELLEY'S GRAVE

cypresses on the other, lies the *Cor Cordium*, forever at rest from the unloving cavillers of this world, whether or not he may have entered on other purifying struggles in some world unseen by us. The grave of Keats lies far off from Shelley's, unshaded by wall or tree. It is painful to look upon, because of the inscription on the stone, which makes him still seem to speak in bitterness from his tomb."

Not far from Shelley's grave, in this Protestant Cemetery, is that of Constance Fenimore Woolson, who died in Venice in January, 1894, and was buried there at her own request.

She was preceded, in 1893, by John Addington Symonds, whose body was carried there by the hands of loving friends, one warm May morning, from the Hotel Italia, where he had passed away in peace.

And she was followed, in the early autumn of 1895, by William Wetmore Story, artist in marble as well as in words, who lies with his wife by the side of the ashes of Shelley and of Symonds. He lived for many years in the

Barberini Palace, and he was one of the most important and familiar figures in that quarter of the world of art and letters which lies between the Tiber and the Esquiline Hill. His monument to Mrs. Story was the sculptor's last and perhaps his greatest work, certainly the work in which was put the most of his heart.

Longfellow's first visit to Rome was in the winter of 1828. In 1869, almost half a century later, he wrote: " Here we are at a new hotel built in the gardens of Sallust's villa, on a spur of the Quirinal, back of the Barberini Palace. In the rear the windows look across the Campagna to the Alban Hills. In front we have all Rome, unrolled like a panorama and crowned by St. Peter's. . . . I look out of the window this gray, rainy day [30th January] and see the streets all mud, and the roofs all green mould, and the mist lying like a pall over the lower town. And Rome seems to me like King Lear, staggering in the storm and crowned with weeds. But this is altogether too fine writing!" The house which he thus described was the Ho-

CONSTANCE FENIMORE WOOLSON'S GRAVE

tel Costanzo, now a German Jesuit College, extending from No. 5 to No. 10 Via S. Nicola da Tolentino.

"At Rome," said Sir William Gell, "Sir Walter [Scott] found an apartment provided for him in the Casa Bernini. . . . Soon after his arrival I took him to St. Peter's, which he had resolved to visit that he might see the tomb of the last of the Stuarts." A few days later Scott went to the Villa Muti at Frascati, which once belonged to the Cardinal of York. He was too feeble to see much or to do much in Rome. "I walk with pain," he said, "and what we see whilst suffering makes little impression on us." In his *Journal* he wrote, on the 16th April, 1832: "We entered Rome by a gate renovated by one of the old Pontiffs, but which I forget, and so paraded the streets by moonlight to discover, if possible, some appearance of the learned Sir William Gell or the pretty Mrs. Ashley. At length we found our old servant, who guided us to the lodging taken by Sir William Gell, where all was comfortable, a good fire included, which our fatigue and the chilliness of the night required. We dispersed as soon as we had taken some food, wine, and water.

"We slept reasonably, but on the next morning—" Here the *Journal* stops abruptly, and forever. Lockhart believed these to have been the last words Scott ever penned. And they were penned in Rome!

A tablet marks the house of Scott, which stands in the narrow little Via di Mercede, not far from the General Post-Office.

James Fenimore Cooper first entered Rome "by the Gate of St. John" in the spring of 1838. His earliest stopping-place was at the Hôtel de Paris, in the Via S. Nicolà da Tolentino, but in a short time he occupied lodgings in the Via di Ripetta. He made no notes of Rome which are worthy of record. He saw everything that was to be seen, he enjoyed everything he saw, but he left Rome with little regret.

Hans Christian Andersen made repeated visits to Rome. The first was in 1833, when he saw the second funeral of Raphael, and formed an acquaintance with Thorwaldsen. He was here again in 1841, when his birthday was celebrated, and when he wrote, in *The Story of My Life:* " Frau von Goethe, who was in Rome, and who chanced to be living in the very house where I brought my ' Improvisatore ' into the world, and made him spend his first years of childhood, sent me from thence a large, true Roman bouquet, a fragrant mosaic." In *The Improvisatore* he said: " Whoever has been in Rome is well acquainted with the Piazza Barberini, in the great square, with the beautiful fountain where the Tritons empty the spouting conch-shell, from which the water springs upwards many feet. Whoever has not been there knows it, at all events, from the copper-plate engravings; only it is a pity that in these the house at the corner of the Via Felice is not given—that tall corner house, where the water pours through three pipes out of the wall into the stone basin. That house has a peculiar interest for me; for it was there that I [' The Improvisatore '] was born."

This house, Nos. 1 and 2 Piazza Barberini,

on the northeastern corner of the square and the Via Sistina — once Via Felice — is still pointed out by a few old friends, who remember Andersen as living in it himself. He is said to have occupied rooms on the second story; and his windows, on the floor above the little balcony, looked out upon the Fountain of the Triton and his attending dolphins. The beautiful old fountain on the side of this house is now a thing of the past. From its three pipes flowed, free to all, in Andersen's time, and long before, the delicious Acqua Felice.

In 1861 Andersen wrote: "In the old Café Græce I got apartments for myself and my young travelling companion, and now we went out into the great city, so familiar and so homelike." The Caffè Greco is at No. 86 Via Condotti.

In *What I Remember*, Thomas' Adolphus Trollope wrote: "In the autumn of 1847 my mother and I went to pass the winter in Rome. Our apartment was in a small palazzo in that part of the Via Quattro Fontane which is now situated between the Via

THE HOUSE OF ANDERSEN, PIAZZA BARBERINI

Nazionale and the church of S. Maria Maggiore, to the left of one going towards the latter. . . . It was a very comfortable apartment, roomy, sunny, and quiet. It exists still [1888], though somewhat modernized in outward appearance, and is, I think, the second after one, going towards S. Maria Maggiore, has crossed the new Via Nazionale."

Trollope finally settled in Rome in 1873, and remained here for some fourteen years; living first in the Via Rosella, opposite the Scotch College; then at No. 9 Via Susanna; and later in the Via Nazionale, in a house originally numbered 367, and afterwards 243. This last house remains unchanged.

In the late winter of 1847 Mrs. Jameson lodged at No. 53 Piazza di Spagna. Her niece, and companion, wrote: "Our rooms were over Spithover's shop, with little balconied windows looking out over all the amusing scenes in the Piazza, the sparkling of the great fountain, and the picturesque figures, models, and contadini that group themselves upon the Spanish Steps. . . . Her life in Rome was a very pleasant one while undisturbed by all [domestic] agitations. As she herself wrote, she went nowhere unconnected with her present labors [*The Sacred and Legendary Art*], unless it were occasionally for a long drive, after the day's toil might be considered as over, away into the Campagna." In March, 1847, Mrs. Jameson said: "I have very pleasant *soirées* on Sunday evenings, which are liked; but my room is so small that I cannot have above twenty people, and I give them only tea." She left Rome after Easter, not to return until 1857.

We find her once more in Rome in 1859, when she lived on the third floor of an ancient four-storied house, No. 176 Via di Ripetta, "close by the Tiber side of the Palazzo Borghese." Here she met Gibson the sculptor, the Storys, Miss Hosmer—who pointed out her windows to the present writer—and the Hawthornes. She went to Florence in the spring, and she never saw Rome again. Hawthorne recorded, in his *Italian Note Books*, that " Mrs. Jameson lived on the first piano of an old palazzo on the Via di Ripetta, nearly opposite the ferry-way across the Tiber, and affording a pleasant view of the yellow river and the green bank and fields on the other side."

Mr. Norton prints none of the letters of Lowell written during his visit to Italy in 1852, when he lost a little son in Rome; but in 1874 Lowell spent a fortnight with Mr. and Mrs. Story in the Palazzo Barberini; and in 1881 he was at the Hotel Bristol. "My windows," he said, "look out on one side towards the Barberini, and on the other towards the old Triton; the weather is fine as fine can be, and I do nothing with commendable assiduity—thawing myself out in the sun like a winter fly. . . . The only costumes left now are on the brazen-faced models, and one sees below—what? Those hateful boots with high heels in the midst of the sole, on which they tottle about as on pegtops. When I was first here every peasant woman wore sandals. I always hated those eternal representations of women with dirty towels on their heads, which express the highest aspiration and conviction of modern art—but this is like the cloven hoof."

In January, 1854, Mrs. Browning wrote from "43 Via di Bocca di Leone, 3d piano. We have pleasant music at Mrs. Sartoris's once or twice a week, and have Fanny Kemble come in to talk to us, with the doors shut, we three together. This is pleasant. If anybody wants small-talk by handfuls, of glittering dust swept out of *salons*, here's Mr. Thackeray besides!" Later she wrote: "We have met Lockhart, and my husband sees a good deal of him. Robert went down to the sea-side, on a day's excursion with him and the Sartorises—and, I hear, found favor in his sight. Said the critic, 'I like Browning—he isn't at all like a damned literary man!' That's a compliment, I believe!"

Mrs. Ritchie possesses a letter written by Mrs. Browning to Thackeray dated "28 Via del Tritone, Rome, 13th April," but unfortunately without the year. In her *Records of Browning* she writes: "In the winter of 1853-54 we [the Thackerays] lived in Rome, in the Via del Croce, and the Brownings lived in the Bocca di Leone, hard by. The evenings our father dined away from home our old donna would conduct us to our tranquil dissipations, through the dark streets, past the swinging lamps, up and down the black stone staircases; and very often we spent an evening with Mrs. Browning in her quiet room, while Mr. Browning was out visiting some of the many friends who were assembled in Rome that year."

The Via di Bocca di Leone is a narrow street, and the rooms of the Brownings, pointed out by Miss Hosmer, who knew them there, had but little sun in the front, although, no doubt, the rear was warmer and more cheerful. Later they were at No. 113—now No. 37—Via del Tritone, as Miss Hosmer remembers, in a house very much changed since their occupancy of it. The street has been re-numbered in a most confusing way; and both the old and the new numbers are still to be seen; the old are in red figures; the new are in figures cut into the houses themselves.

A favorite stopping-place of Thackeray

was the Hotel Inghilterra, a hostelry still standing, and unchanged, in the Via di Bocca di Leone. And here he is said to have written *The Rose and the Ring*, for Mr. Story's little daughter, reading it to her, chapter by chapter, as it was composed.

"At seven o'clock," said Hawthorne, 22d May, 1858, " we went by invitation to take tea with Miss Bremer. After much search, and lumbering up two or three staircases in vain, and at last going about in a strange circuity, we found her in a small chamber of a large old building situated a little way from the brow of the Tarpeian Rock. It was the tiniest and humblest domicile that I have seen in Rome, just large enough to hold her narrow bed, her tea-table, and a table covered with books—photographs of Roman ruins—and some pages written by herself. I wonder whether she is poor. Probably so; for she told us that her expense of living here is only five pauls a day. . . . Meanwhile as the day declined there had been the most beautiful view over the Campagna from one of her windows;

and from the other, looking towards St. Peter's, the broad gleam of a mildly glorious sunset. . . . In the garden beneath her window, verging upon the Tarpeian Rock, there was shrubbery and one large tree, softening the brow of the famous precipice down which the Old Romans used to fling their traitors, or sometimes indeed their patriots."

When Motley first came to Rome he lived in the Palazzo Bernini, No. 151 Via del Corso. Later and longer he lived on the second floor of the Palazzo Zuccari, No. 64 Via Sistina. In 1858 he wrote to his mother: " We are now in very comfortable lodgings on the Corso, about opposite the Church of S. Carlo, if you happen to remember it. We are on the third floor. . . . I have a good room for my study, and I am hard at work. I began my first volume about a fortnight ago, and hope to have it done by April. . . . I have to spread myself over a wide surface, for after the death of William the Silent the history of the province becomes, for a time, swallowed up in the general current of European history. I do not mean by that that it loses its importance. On the contrary, the Netherlands question becomes the great question of history."

George Eliot and Lewes first saw Rome in the spring of 1860. According to her own statement she lived at "the Hotel Inghilterra in the Strada Babuino," which leads directly from the Piazza del Popolo to the Piazza di Spagna; but as the Hôtel d'Amérique was in this street, and the Hotel Inghilterra in another part of the town, she must have confused the names. The Amérique was the building now numbered 78 and 79 Via del Babuino, and it is no longer a hotel. Old friends of hers still remember her at this house.

"Discontented with our little room at an extravagant height of stairs and price," she wrote, "we found, and took, lodgings the next day in the Corso, opposite S. Carlo, with a well-mannered Frenchman and his little dark Italian wife—and so felt ourselves settled for a month." "Yesterday" (3d April), she wrote to Mrs. Congreve, "was taken up with seeing ceremonies, or rather waiting for them. I knelt down to receive the Pope's blessing, remembering what Pius VII. said to the soldier — that one would never be the worse for the blessing of an old man."

Mr. J. W. Cross recorded in his *Life of George Eliot* that he first met that lady in May, 1869, at the Hotel Minerva here, where Lewes had taken rooms. And he spoke of "the low, deep, earnest musical tones of her voice, of the fine brows with the abundant auburn-brown hair framing them, of the long head broadening at the back, of the gray-blue eyes, constantly changing in expression, but always with a very loving, almost deprecating look at the lady with whom she was speaking, of the finely formed, thin, transparent hands, and a whole *Wesen* that seemed in complete harmony with everything one expected to find in the author of *Romola*."

The Hotel Minerva is No. 69 Piazza della Minerva.

"We spent three delightful winters in Rome," said Locker-Lampson, "arriving at the Piazza di Spagna, No. 31, on the 29th December, 1861; at No. 103 Via de' Due Macelli on the 17th December, 1862; and lastly, at No. 43 Via di Bocca di Leone 2° p° (I specify it all with amorous precision) on the 17th November, 1866." But he specified nothing of the life he lived here, except a list of the persons he met, and the fact that for a portion of the time he " filled the high office of warden to the Episcopal Church immediately outside the Porta del Popolo."

Lord Houghton lived at No. 8 Via S. Basilio, in a house later the residence of George P. Marsh. Afterwards he was a guest at the Hôtel de Londres, in the Piazza di Spagna.

George P. Marsh dwelt at No. 8 Via S. Basilio, on the floor above the ground-floor. Later he lived in the Piazza dell' Esquilino, in the house where are now displayed the arms of the Argentine Republic; and during the last few years of his residence in Rome he had an apartment in the Palazzo Rospigliosi, on the Quirinal Hill, near the Via Nazionale. He was buried in the Protestant Cemetery in 1882.

The only picture Dean Stanley gave of his personal experiences in Rome is in a letter written in October, 1866, from 51 Piazza di Spagna. "We have moved here," he wrote, "from our hotel. The Gladstones were so kindly urgent about it, and the advantages of the situation so great, that we determined to try the experiment, and it completely answers. They are on the second, we on the third floor. The dining-room is on the third floor, and we have hitherto always dined together. This is the only time when we necessarily meet; but very pleasant it is. He [Gladstone] is so extremely enjoying his liberty." That the gentle dean enjoyed his own liberty extremely during his stay in Rome is evident in everything he wrote about it to his friends at home.

Mrs. Helen Hunt rested in the winter of 1868-69, between her *Bits of Travel*, at No. 155 Via Quattro Fontane — "just opposite the Barberini, on the corner opposite Miss Hosmer's house. Think of that! Aren't we in luck?" She wrote to her "Dear Souls" at home: "The rooms are charming — a parlor on the southeast corner, two windows; a dining-room, two bedrooms, and such a kitchen, resplendent with copper."

Louisa Alcott occupied, in the winter of 1870–71, an apartment on the northeastern corner of the Via S. Nicolà da Tolentino and the Piazza Barberini; and it must have been an awkward address to put on the visiting-cards she had to leave, no doubt, as is the Roman way, upon every person she wished to have call upon her. It takes a month or two in Rome to master the etiquette of calls and of cards, and even then the stranger is apt to leave the wrong card and to make the wrong call. But this has nothing to do with Miss Alcott. Her house, an old, tumble-down, two-and-a-half-storied edifice, was taken to pieces, in self-defence, a few years ago; and a fine, square, many-windowed, modern building now occupies its site. In November, 1870, she wrote in her *Journal:*

"In Rome; and felt as if I had been there before, and knew all about it. Always depressed with a sense of sin, dirt, and general decay of all things. Not well; so saw things through blue glasses. . . . Our apartment in the Piazza Barberini was warm and cozy; and I thanked Heaven for it, as it rained for two months, and my first view most of the time was the poor Triton with an icicle on his nose." The next year, still in Rome, she wrote: "Began to write a new book, *Little Men*, that John's death may not leave A—— and the dear little boys in want."

Miss Amelia B. Edwards once had rooms in the house where lodged Miss Alcott.

On the 22d November, 1870, Mary Howitt wrote to her daughter: "We are located on the summit of one of the Seven Hills, at a corner of four converging streets, each visibly terminating by an historic monument." Later she wrote: "We are located in charming new quarters—in the Via di Porta Pinciani." In 1871 they were in the Via Sistina, No. 55. "Looking up the street," she said, "the Piazza of the Trinità de' Monti immediately opens before us, with the distant heights of Monte Mario, where the sun now sets and the evening skies are beautiful. Just opposite to us is the old palace of some Queen of Poland, a rather dingy-looking place, with traces of grandeur about it. It forms a division between the Via Sistina and the Via Gregoriana, which unite in the Piazza." Here William Howitt died in 1879.

In May of the same year Mrs. Howitt moved for a few weeks into apartments at No. 86 Via Sistina. In 1887 she wrote from No. 38 Via Gregoriana: "We are in what was Miss Charlotte Cushman's Roman home." And here she died in January of the next year. She was buried in the Protestant Cemetery by her husband's side.

Hawthorne has told the story of his life in Rome very thoroughly in his *Italian Note Books*, which, if they were properly indexed, would be the best guides to Rome ever published. They should be read before one goes to Rome, while one is in Rome, and after one has left Rome; and then they should be read again and again. And *The Marble Faun* should receive the same close and studious attention.

Two of Hawthorne's dwelling-places in Rome are still remembered by some of his old friends here; and there is a pleasant tradition—unverified, however, by anything recorded in his *Journals* or his *Letters*—that he at one time occupied the rooms with the balcony, on the northeastern corner of the Via Sistina and the Piazza Barberini, directly beneath what was once the home of Hans Christian Andersen.

From "No. 37 Palazzo Larazani, Via di Porta Pinciana, 24th January, 1858," he wrote: "After a day or two we settled ourselves in a suite of ten rooms, comprehending one flat, on what is called the second piano of this house. The rooms thus far have been very uncomfortable, it being impossible to warm them by means of the deep, old-fashioned, artificial fireplaces unless we had the great logs of a New England forest to burn in them, so I have sat in my corner by the fireside with more clothes on than I ever wore before, and my thickest great-coat over all."

The Hawthornes, having spent some time in Florence, came back to Rome in October, 1858, and they lived, until they left Italy in the month of May, 1859, at No. 68 Piazza Poli. "We have the snuggest little suite of apartments in Rome. Seven rooms, including an antechamber; and though the stairs are exceedingly narrow, there is really a carpet on them—a civilized comfort of which the proudest palaces in the Eternal City cannot boast. The stairs are very steep, however, and I should not wonder if some of us broke our noses on them. . . . Our windows here look out on a small and rather quiet piazza, with an immense palace on the left hand, and a smaller yet statelier one on the right; and just round the corner of the street leading out of our piazza is the Fountain of Trevi, of which I can hear the plash in the evening, when other sounds are hushed."

The Piazza Poli house is no longer standing. Its site is now occupied by what seems to be the Sunday-school room, or office, of the Methodist Church, Nos. 2 and 3 Via Poli. The entire appearance of that particular quarter of the town has been changed.

Here it was that *The Marble Faun*, that famous romance which the English for some unknown reason call *Transformation*, was conceived; and Hawthorne's own identification of the Marble Faun itself will interest many of its admirers.

In 1860 he wrote to Henry Bright: "You will not find any photograph or (so far as I am aware) any engraving of the Faun of Praxiteles. There are photographs, stereoscopic and otherwise, of another Faun which is almost identical with the hero of my romance, although only an inferior repetition of it. My Faun is in the Capitol; the other in the Vatican. The genuine statue has never been photographed, on account, I suppose, of its standing in a bad light. The photographs of the Vatican Faun supply its place very well, except as to the face, which is very inferior."

Hawthorne, in his own inimitable way, painted the picture of Hilda's Tower, in the sixth chapter of the romance. "Connected with this old tower," he said, "is a legend which we cannot pause here to tell; but for centuries a lamp has been burning before the Virgin's image, at noon, at midnight, and at all hours of the twenty-four; and must be kept burning forever, as long as the tower shall stand; or else the tower itself, the palace, and whatever estate belongs to it shall pass from its hereditary possessor, in accordance with an ancient vow, and become the property of the Church."

The Church is not so powerful in Rome as it was in 1859, when Hawthorne wrote, but the lamp still burns, and the legend which he could not pause to tell in *The Marble Faun* he has told in his *Note Books*, and it is well worth repeating here in full: "Mr. [Cephas G.] Thompson took me into the Via Portoghesi, and showed me an old palace, about which rose — not a very customary feature of the architecture of Rome — a tall, battlemented tower. At one angle

HILDA'S TOWER

of the tower we saw a shrine of the Virgin, with a lamp and all the appendages of those numerous shrines which we see at the street corners and in hundreds of places about the city. Three or four centuries ago this palace was inhabited by a nobleman who had an only son and a large pet monkey, and one day the monkey caught the infant up, and clambered to this lofty turret, and sat there, with him in his arms, grinning and chattering like the devil himself. The father was in despair, but was afraid to pursue the monkey lest he should fling down the child from the height of the tower and make his escape. At last he vowed that if the boy were safely restored to him he would build a shrine at the summit of the tower, and cause it to be kept as a sacred place forever. By-and-by the monkey came down, and deposited the child on the ground; the father fulfilled his vow, built the shrine, and made it obligatory on all future possessors of the place to keep the lamp burning before it."

Hilda's Tower is beautiful in itself, and well worth a visit for its own sake. It stands, in its square and rugged solidity, two stories above the large house of which it forms a corner. A fine old projecting gateway leads into a small court-yard, which, when the present pilgrim last saw it, one Christmas Eve, had never a dove, but was occupied by dismal chickens and dismal children, and ragged clothes hung out to dry. It can be found in an out-of-the-way corner of the Rome of to-day, in the short little Via Portoghesi, west of the Corso; and one wonders, as one goes towards it by a most winding route from "The Strangers' Quarter," or from the Quirinal Hill, how Hilda or Hawthorne came upon it at all. The little shrine to the Virgin and the lamp which illumines it so faintly at night can easily be seen from the street. The people of its neighborhood who gaze upon it know, and care, more about the legend of the baby and the monkey than they do about the story which Hawthorne so touchingly told; but it is one of the most precious of the Literary Landmarks of Rome; and it seems particularly fitting that American and

English readers should say, in these pages, "good-night" to Rome, by the light of the lantern dimly burning on the summit of Hilda's Tower.

INDEX OF PERSONS

ALCOTT, LOUISA, 58–59.
Andersen, Hans Christian, 44–46, 61.

BREMER, FREDERIKA, 52–53.
Browning, Elizabeth Barrett, 50–51.
Browning, Robert, 50–51.
Byron, Lord, 31–32.
Byron, Lord, quoted, 8.

CÆSAR, JULIUS, 4, 5–11.
Châteaubriand, 27–28.
Cherbury, Lord Herbert of, 18.
Cicero, 4–5.
Cooper, James Fenimore, 44.
Cross, J. W., quoted, 55.
Cushman, Charlotte, 60.

DANTE, 18.
Dickens, Charles, quoted, 34–35.
Dionysius, quoted, 29.

EDWARDS, AMELIA B., 59.
"Eliot, George," 54–55.
"Eliot, George," quoted, 40–41.

Evans, Mary Anne, 54–55.
Evans, Mary Anne, quoted, 40–41.
Evelyn, John, 24–25.

FORBES, S. RUSSELL, quoted, 4, 6, 7, 13, 29, 39.

GALILEO, 21–22.
"George Eliot," 54–55.
"George Eliot," quoted, 40–41.
Gladstone, William Ewart, 57.
Goethe, 26–27, 31.
Gray, Thomas, 25.

HARE, AUGUSTUS J. C., quoted, 4, 8, 16.
Hawthorne, Nathaniel, 48, 60–67.
Hawthorne, Nathaniel, quoted, 9–10, 23, 48–49, 52–53.
Herbert, Lord (of Cherbury), 18.
Hillard, George S., quoted, 22–23, 27–28.
Horace, 12–13.
Hosmer, Harriet, 33, 48, 51, 58.

Houghton, Lord, 56.
Houghton, Lord, quoted, 37.
Howitt, Mary, 59–60.
Howitt, William, 59–60.
Hunt, Helen, 57–58.

JAMESON, ANNA, 47–49.

KEATS, JOHN, 32, 33–38, 39, 41.
Kemble, Fanny, 50.
Knowles, James Sheridan, quoted, 28.

LANCIANI, RODOLFO, quoted, 4, 10, 13.
Lewes, George Henry, 54–55.
Locker-Lampson, Frederick, 55–56.
Lockhart, John Gibson, 44, 50.
Lockhart, John Gibson, quoted, 44.
Longfellow, Henry Wadsworth, 42–43.
Lowell, James Russell, 49–50.
Lucullus, 5.
Luther, Martin, 15–17.

MACAULAY, LORD, 29–30.
Mæcenas, 12, 13.
Marsh, George P., 56–57.
Middleton, J. Henry, quoted, 4, 12.
Milton, John, 22–24.
Montaigne, 18–20.
Motley, John Lothrop, 53–54.

PEDO ALBINOVANUS, 13.
Petrarch, 13–14.
Pliny, 13.

RITCHIE, ANNE THACKERAY, quoted, 50–51.
Rogers, Samuel, 30–31.

SALLUST, 11–12.
Scott, Walter, 43–44.
Severn, Joseph, 32, 37.
Severn, Joseph, quoted, 35–37.
Shelley, Percy Bysshe, 32, 38–41.
Shelley, Percy Bysshe, quoted, 37.
Smollett, Tobias, 26.
Staël, Madame de, 30.
Stanley, Arthur Penrhyn, 57.
Story, William Wetmore, 41–42, 48, 49, 52.
Symonds, John Addington, 41.

TASSO, 20–21.
Thackeray, William Makepeace, 50, 51–52.
Trollope, Frances M., 46–47.
Trollope, Thomas Adolphus, 46–47.

VIRGIL, 12.

WALPOLE, HORACE, 25–26.
Wilson, Francis, 21.
Woolson, Constance Fenimore, 41.

INDEX OF PLACES

Alban Hill, 21, 42.
Amérique, Hôtel, 54.
Andrea, S., della Valle, Church, 7.
Appian Way, 5.
Argiletum, 13.
Augustine Convent, 15–16.

Babuino, Via, 54.
Barberini, Palazzo, 23, 42, 49, 58, 61.
Barberini, Piazza, 45, 49, 58, 59, 61.
Barberini, Villa, 12.
Basilio, S., Via, 56 *bis*.
Baths of Titus, 13.
Bear Hotel, 17–18, 19.
Bernini, Casa, 43–44.
Bernini, Palazzo, 53.
Bocca di Leone, Via di, 50–51, 52, 56.
Borghese, Palazzo, 48.
Bristol, Hotel, 49.

Cæsar, Temple of, 10, 29.
Caius Cestius, Pyramid of, 36–37.
Campagna, 42, 52.
Capena, Porta, 5.

Capitol, 63.
Capitol Hill, 14.
Capo di Ferro, Piazza, 7.
Carlo, S., Church, 53, 54.
Carrozza, Via, 32.
Cemetery, English, 36–38, 39, 40–41, 57.
Churches—
 Andrea, S., della Valle, 7.
 Carlo, S., 53, 54.
 Lateran, S. John, 19–20.
 Lucia, S., della Tinta, 19.
 Maria, S., del Popolo, 16.
 Peter, S., 43.
 Trinità, S., de' Monti, 33.
Cicero's Villa, 4–5.
Cœlius, Mount, 30.
Colosseum, 9.
Condotti, Via, 46.
Corso, Via del, 26, 31, 39, 53, 54.
Corso Vittorio Emanuele, Via, 7.
Costanzo, Hotel, 42–43.
Croce, Via del, 50.
Curia, 5, 8.

Due Macelli, Via de', 56.

English Cemetery, 36-38, 39, 40-41, 57.
Esquiline Hill, 12, 13, 42.
Esquilino, Piazza dell', 56.

Farnese, Palazzo, 24.
Felice, Via, 45-46.
Forum, 5, 6, 10-11, 13.
Frascati, 43.

Giovanni, S., Porta, 44.
Greco, Caffè, 46.
Gregoriana, Via, 60.
Grotta Ferrata, 4-5.

Hilda's Tower, 64-67.
Hills—
  Alban, 21, 42.
  Capitol, 14,
  Cœlius, 30.
  Esquiline, 12, 13, 42.
  Janiculum, 20.
  Mario, 60.
  Palatine, 4, 30, 32.
  Pincian, 5, 12.
  Quirinal, 12, 42-43, 56.
  Sabine, 21.
  Sacer, 29.
Holy Staircase, 16-17.
Hotels—
  Amérique, 54.
  Bear, 17-18, 19.
  Bristol, 49.
  Costanzo, 42-43.
  Inghilterra, 52, 54.
  Italia, 41.
  Londres, 56.
  Minerva, 55.
  Orso, 17-18, 19.
  Paris, 44.

Indipendenza, Piazza dell', 31.
Inghilterra, Hotel, 52, 54.
Italia, Hotel, 41.

Janiculum Hill, 20.
Julia, Rostra, 10.
Jupiter Stator, Temple of, 4.

Larazani, Palazzo, 61-62.
Lateran, S. John, Church, 19-20.
Londres, Hôtel de, 56.
Lucia, S., della Tinta, Church, 19.
Lucullus, Villa of, 5.

Mæcenas, Villa of, 12-13.
Magenta, Via, 31.
Maria, S., de' Fiori, Via, 31.
Maria, S., Maggiore, Via, 13, 47.
Maria, S., sopra Minerva, Convent, 21-22.
Maria, S., del Popolo, Church, 16.
Mario, Monte, 60.
Mercede, Via di, 44.
Mills, Villa, 32.
Minerva, Hotel, 55.
Minerva, Piazza della, 22, 55.

Muti, Villa, 43.

NAZIONALE, VIA, 46–47, 56–57.
Nicola, S., da Tolentino, Via, 43, 44, 58–59.

ONOFRIO, S., MONASTERY, 20–21.
Orso, Albergo dell', 17–18, 19.
Orso, Via dell', 17.

PALATINE HILL, 4, 30, 32.
Palazzo—
  Barberini, 23, 42, 49, 58, 61.
  Bernini, 53.
  Borghese, 48.
  Farnese, 24.
  Larazani, 61–62.
  Quirinal, 23.
  Rondinini, 27, 31.
  Rospigliosa, 56.
  Spada alla Regola, 7–10.
  Verospi, 39.
  Zuccari, 53–54.
Paolo, S. Porta, 40.
Paris, Hôtel de, 44.
Peter, S., Cathedral, 43.
Pia, Porta, 23, 29.
Piazza—
  Barberini, 45, 49, 58, 59, 61.
  Capo di Ferro, 7.
  Esquilino, 56.
  Indipendenza, 31.
  Minerva, 22, 55.

Poli, 62–63.
Popolo, 26, 54.
Spagna, 24, 26, 32, 33–36, 38–39, 47–48, 54, 56 *bis*, 57.
Trinità, S., de Monti, 59–60.
Pincian Hill, 5, 12.
Poli, Piazza, 62–63.
Poli, Via, 63.
Pompey's Senate House, 7.
Pompey's Statue, 7–10.
Pompey's Theatre, 7.
Ponte—
  Rotto, 30.
  Sublicius, 30.
Popolo, Piazza del, 26, 54.
Popolo, Porta del, 25, 56.
Porta—
  Capena, 5.
  Giovanni, S., 44.
  Paolo, S., 40.
  Pia, 23, 29.
  Popolo, 25, 56.
Porta Pinciani, Via di, 59, 61.
Portoghesi, Via, 64–67.
Post-Office, General, 44.
Protestant Cemetery, 36–38, 39, 40–41, 57.
Pyramid of Caius Cestius, 36–37.

QUATTRO FONTANE, VIA, 23, 46–47, 57–58.
Quirinal Hill, 12, 42–43, 56.
Quirinal Palace, 23.

REGIA, 6.
Ripetta, Via di, 44, 48-49.
Rondinini, Palazzo, 27, 31.
Rosella, Via, 47.
Rospigliosi, Palazzo, 56.
Rostra, 5.
Rostra, Julia, 10.
Rotto, Ponte, 30.

SABINE HILLS, 21.
Sacer, Mons, 29.
Sacra, Via, 6-7, 29.
Sacred Way, 6-7, 29.
Sallust, Villa of, 11-12, 42.
Scala, Santa, 16-17.
Senate Hall, 14.
Senate House, Pompey's, 7.
Shrine of Venus, 28-29.
Sistina, Via, 46, 53, 60, 61.
Spada alla Regola, Palazzo, 7-10.
Spagna, Piazza di, 24, 26, 32, 33-36, 38-39, 47-48, 54, 56 *bis*, 57.
Spanish Steps, 33, 38-39, 47.
Stranger's Quarter, 24, 26, 32, 33-36, 38-39, 47-48, 54, 56 *bis*, 57.
Sublician Bridge, 30.
Suburra, 13.
Susanna, Via, 47.

TARPEIAN ROCK, 52-53.
Tasso's Oak, 21.
Temple—
  of Cæsar, 10, 29.
  of Jupiter Stator, 4.
  of Vesta, 6.

Theatre of Pompey, 7.
Titus, Baths of, 13.
Trinità, S., de' Monti, Church, 33.
Trinità, S., de' Monti, Piazza, 59-60.
Tritone, Via del, 50, 51.
Tusculum, 4-5.

VATICAN, 63.
Venus, Shrine of, 28-29.
Verospi, Palazzo, 39.
Vesta, Temple of, 6.
Via—
  Babuino, 54.
  Basilio, S., 56 *bis*.
  Bocca di Leone, 50-51, 52, 56.
  Carrozza, 32.
  Condotti, 46.
  Corso, 26, 31, 39, 53, 54.
  Corso Vittorio Emanuele, 7.
  Croce, 50.
  Due Macelli, 56.
  Felice, 45-46.
  Gregoriana, 60.
  Magenta, 31.
  Maria, S., de' Fiori, 31.
  Maria, S., Maggiore, 13, 47.
  Mercede, 44.
  Nazionale, 46-47, 56-57.
  Nicolà, S., da Tolentino, 43, 44, 58-59.
  Orso, 17.
  Poli, 63.
  Porta Pinciani, 59, 61.
  Portoghesi, 64-67.

Quattro Fontane, 23, 46–47, 57–58.
Ripetta, 44, 48–49.
Rosella, 47.
Sacra, 6–7, 29.
Sistina, 46, 53, 60, 61.
Susanna, 47.
Tritone, 50, 51.
Vittoria, 31.
Vicus Cyprius, 13.
Vicus Tuscus, 28–29.

Villa—
  Barberini, 12.
  Cicero, 4–5.
  Lucullus, 5.
  Mæcenas, 12–13.
  Mills, 32.
  Muti, 43.
  Sallust, 11–12, 42.
Vittoria, Via, 31.

ZUCCARRI, PALAZZO, 53–54.

THE END

www.ingramcontent.com/pod-product-compliance
Lightning Source LLC
Chambersburg PA
CBHW020150170426
43199CB00010B/975